Mary Chapin Carpenter
Stones In The Road

Foreword

The magic of the world of song, Mary Chapin Carpenter has said, "is that there's the recognition. Someone's experiencing something in their own life, and you hear it articulated in a song and you just recognize it. It's like hearing a bell ring—it's unmistakable—and you can't help but be changed."

In a short period of time, Carpenter has become a widely respected and major creative force in contemporary music. She is someone who rings the recognition bell in us often, whether it's examining the existential loneliness in our lives ("John Doe No. 24") or questioning the ideals of a generation wounded by assassination, riots and social upheaval ("Stones In The Road").

Her audience is drawn to her by the substance and integrity of her work, and she has been able to build her career without compromising content and without the bombast and hype that so often accompany her level of achievement.

Stones In The Road is her fifth album for Columbia Records and contains 13 new songs written by Carpenter. Its release in October 1994 marked the end of nearly a year's hiatus from touring so that she could concentrate on writing the record. "If there are people who can write great songs on the road, my hat's off to them," says Carpenter. "I need to be at my desk for concentrated periods of time."

Her need for time at home to write became one of the central frustrations during the 18 months she was out touring behind *Come On Come On*, an album that had an unprecedented seven Top Twenty singles and has sold over 3 million copies, and which earned two Grammys for Mary Chapin and one for Lucinda Williams (the writer of "Passionate Kisses"). "I remember one day realizing that I hadn't written anything for as long as I could remember," she says. "Between the recording of and touring behind *Come On Come On*, it was nearly two years and it was scary ... that somehow the momentum of a record was keeping me from doing the very thing that started me doing this in the first place: expressing myself, songwriting. ..."

Understanding her need for time to

write, Carpenter spent from November 1993 through June 1994 working on new songs for *Stones In The Road*; all of the songs on the record were written during that time, save for the album's title track. "Stones In The Road" was to have been on *Come On Come On*, Carpenter explains, "but I was doing a benefit with Joan Baez and the Indigo Girls before we started recording it. Joan asked me if she could record the song for her album, and I agreed that hers would be the first version released. Her record got delayed so we ended up not putting it on mine, knowing that we could use it later."

Says Carpenter of the forces at work in her life and writing, "I think it's not so much about changing the world, but how your world changes. In the midst of chasing the golden ring, you get backslapped and you start to question your priorities. The further you go, the more you see ... and in the end, your needs come down to the basics: time for yourself, your family, honest relationships, and giving to each other. The time you give to these things is the most precious thing there is.

"When I write, the songs acknowledge some of the dark places and some of the dark times. But I don't think it's a negative, because you can't know the light without the darkness," she continues. "Somebody once said they like to sing sad songs because it makes them feel brave; I agree and I think it sets you up to see the light clearly and follow it."

Another strength of Carpenter's writing is that she doesn't rely solely on lyrics to engage her audience. Her songs derive their beauty and lyricism from their melodies as well as their words, and from the fluid production which she and long-time producer John Jennings flesh from the songs. Be it the gently rolling piano overture of "Why Walk When You Can Fly" that dissolves into her a cappella vocal; the bluesy "Shut Up And Kiss Me" with Lee Roy Parnell's swampy slide guitar; the Celtic flavorings of Paul Brady's tin whistles on "Jubilee"; or "John Doe No. 24," a startling portrait of a deaf, blind mute strung through an emotional time warp and colored by Branford Marsalis' ethereal soprano sax solos, it is the subtle nuances—lyrical and melodic—that heighten the impact of Carpenter's acute perception of the world.

"I'm as typical a person as they come," Carpenter says. "I'm so much like everyone and we all go through so much that's the same. I try to write what I write and believe that it's true for a lot of people. The challenge is being true to what you feel and to keep doing what you do without worrying about whether you get to Number One.

"With this collection, I want people to feel as though they are on a journey with ups and downs, highs and lows, a sense of tension and relief, and, ultimately, peace within. I took a year off and I really concentrated on writing, which, after being on the road more or less for five years, felt like a real luxury. I've never felt like this before about a body of songs—and it's wonderful. I just hope other people feel it too."

Management:
Tom Carrico and John L. Simson/Studio One Artists
Piano/Vocal Arrangements:
Edwin McLean and John Nicholas
Music Engraving:
Edwin McLean and Gordon Hallberg
Production:
Daniel Rosenbaum and Rana Bernhardt
Art Direction:
Rosemary Cappa-Jenkins and Art Brooks
Director of Music: Mark Phillips

Photography by
Caroline Greyshock

Contents

Lyrics

Why Walk When You Can Fly

Words and Music by Mary Chapin Carpenter

In this world there's a whole lot of trouble baby / In this world there's a whole lot of pain / In this world there's a whole lot of trouble but / A whole lot of ground to gain / Why take when you could be giving / Why watch as the world goes by / It's a hard enough life to be living / Why walk when you can fly

In this world there's a whole lot of sorrow / In this world there's a whole lot of shame / In this world there's a whole lot of sorrow / And a whole lot of ground to gain / When you spend your whole life wishing / Wanting and wondering why / It's a long enough life to be living / Why walk when you can fly

And in this world there's a whole lot of golden / In this world there's a whole lot of plain / In this world you've a soul for a compass / And a heart for a pair of wings / There's a star on the far horizon / Rising bright in an azure sky / For the rest of the time that you're given / Why walk when you can fly high

House Of Cards

Words and Music by Mary Chapin Carpenter

I grew up in a house like this / You knew the groan of every stair / All the walls seemed to listen in / All the years seemed to take up air / And when you dreamed it was of the wind blowing cold and hard / And in those dreams you thought you lived in a house of cards

And I grew up in a town like this / You knew the names of every street / On the surface it looked so safe / But it was perilous underneath / That's the place where you shoved your doubts and hid your ugly scars / God forbid if word got out about your house of cards

And now I feel the wind about to blow / Baby I'm so scared / We're repeating the past instead of letting it go / And I don't want to go back there

Now we're standing here face to face / Afraid to move or else / I want to prop up this fragile place / But I can't do it all by myself / Cause when we dream it's of the wind blowing cold and hard / And when we wake up we still live in a house of cards / When we dream it's of the wind blowing cold and hard / And when we wake up we still live in a house of cards

Stones In The Road

Words and Music by Mary Chapin Carpenter

When we were young we pledged allegiance every morning of our lives / The classroom rang with children's voices under teacher's watchful eye / We learned about the world around us, at our desks and at dinner time / Reminded of the starving children, we cleaned our plates with guilty minds / And the stones in the road, shone like diamonds in the dust / And then a voice called to us to make our way back home

When I was ten my father held me on his shoulders above the crowd / To see a train draped in mourning pass slowly through our town / His widow kneeled with all their children at the sacred burial ground / And the TV glowed that long hot summer with all the cities burning down / And the stones in the road, flew out beneath our bicycle tires / Worlds removed from all those fires as we raced each other home

And now we drink our coffee on the run / We climb that ladder rung by rung / We are the daughters and the sons and here's the line that's missing

The starving children have been replaced by souls out on the street / We give a dollar when we pass and hope our eyes don't meet / We pencil in, we cancel out, we crave the corner suite / We kiss your ass, we make you hold, we doctor the receipt / And the stones in the road fly out from beneath our wheels / Another day, another deal before we get back home / And the stones in the road leave a mark whence they came / A thousand points of light or shame Baby, I don't know

A Keeper For Every Flame

Words and Music by Mary Chapin Carpenter

She says it's been so long she can't remember when / The mention of his name didn't make her feel again / That everything is possible and every day a brand new start / Yeah love's something powerful when it finds a willing heart / Sometimes it's a fire burning out of control / Sometimes it's a candle burning long and low / All these years she never let it go / There's a keeper for every flame

There was someone in his past that he hasn't gotten over yet / Each day's like the last, he just misses what he can't forget / It's just an empty space where something used to be / Now he guards the gate but he's lost the key / So no one enters but no one leaves / There's a keeper for every flame

I thought my heart had broken but it was just a little bruised / I thought love had spoken, guess I was just confused / Sometimes we were a fire burning out of control / Sometimes we were nothing but a candle glow / But it never died baby and how I know / There's a keeper for every flame

Tender When I Want To Be

Words and Music by Mary Chapin Carpenter

I have a heart that's proud you bet / I have a mind that won't forget / And I have arms that are strong and yet / Tender when they want to be / Well you can be the will that finds the way / And you can be the one that saves the day / But show me tender when it's time to say / Exactly how it ought to be

And I never would have known it darling / If I hadn't known about you / You said everyone can be a rock and roll like a river too

Well something happens when you find someone / Who makes you feel like you can do no wrong / No you don't have to take the whole world on / Just be tender when you want to be

And I never would have known it baby / If I hadn't known about you / You said everyone can be a rock and roll like a river too

So let the waters carry us away / Wave goodbye to the old parade / Baby when we're unafraid / To be tender when we want to be / All the waters wash our cares away / All that we can see are better days / Don't ever let me hesitate / To be tender when I want to be

Shut Up And Kiss Me

Words and Music by
Mary Chapin Carpenter

Don't mean to get a little forward with you, don't mean to get ahead of where we are / Don't mean to act a little nervous around you, I'm just a little nervous about my heart 'cause / It's been awhile since I felt this feeling that everything that you do gives me / It's been too long since somebody whispered / Shut up and kiss me

Didn't expect to be in this position, didn't expect to have to rise above / My reputation for cynicism, I've been a jaded lady when it comes to love but / Oh baby just to feel this feeling that everything that you do gives me / It's been too long since somebody whispered / Shut up and kiss me / There's something about the silent type attracting me to you / All business baby none of the hype / That no talker can live up to

Come closer baby I can't hear you, just another whisper if you please / Don't worry 'bout the details darlin', you've got the kind of mind I love to read / Talk is cheap and baby time's expensive, so why waste another minute more / Life's too short to be so apprehensive, love's as much the symptom darlin' as the cure / Oh baby when I feel this feeling, it's like genuine voodoo hits me / It's been too long since somebody whispered... / Oh baby I can feel this feeling that everything that you do gives me / It's been too long since somebody whispered / Shut up and kiss me / Shut up and kiss me

The Last Word

Words and Music by Mary Chapin Carpenter

You can have it, I don't want it and when you've got it I'll be gone / It won't matter what you're saying when the damage has all been done / Can't seem to keep the faith / As if that's all I need to do / I'd rather walk away / Than take what belongs to you / You can have it, I don't want it and when you've got it I'll be gone / It won't matter what you're saying when the damage has all been done / Some words will cut you down / Like you were only in the way / Why should I stand this ground / It won't hurt as much to say / You can have it, I don't want it and when you've got it I'll be gone / It won't matter what you're saying when the damage has all been done / Sometimes we're blinded by / The very thing we need to see / I finally realized / You need it more than you need me / You can have it, I don't want it and when you've got it I'll be gone / It won't matter what you're saying when the damage has all been done / The damage has all been done

The End Of My Pirate Days

Words and Music by Mary Chapin Carpenter

The night is soft and silent, new moon at my door / There's nothing near as quiet as the light I'm looking for / Last time that it appeared he was lying next to me / Last time I felt this near to whispered ecstasy / And those who need adventure / They can sail the seven seas / And those who search for treasure / They must live on grander dreams / We rose and fell just like the tides, he filled my heart and soul / And I buried all my dreams for someone else to find / In my pirate days

This world is kinder to the kind that won't look back / They are the chosen few, among us now, unbowed somehow / And one day he turned to me and before I took one breath / I would only see his shadow in what light was left / And those who need adventure / They can sail the seven seas / And those who search for treasure / They must live on grander dreams / And if I've seen his face since then it's only been in dreams my friend / Since I came to the end of my pirate days / And if I've called his name since then, it's only been in dreams my friend / And so I came to the end of my pirate days

John Doe No. 24

Words and Music by Mary Chapin Carpenter

I was standing on this sidewalk in 1945 in Jacksonville, Illinois / When asked what my name was there came no reply / They said I was a deaf and sightless half-wit boy / But Lewis was my name though I could not say it / I was born and raised in New Orleans / My spirit was wild so I let the river take it / On a barge and a prayer upstream

They searched for a mother and they searched for a father / And they searched 'til they searched no more / The doctors put to rest their scientific tests / And they named me John Doe No. 24 / And they all shook their heads in pity / For a world so silent and dark / Well there's no doubt that life's a mystery / But so too is the human heart

And it was my heart's own perfume when the crape jasmine bloomed on St. Charles Avenue / Though I couldn't hear the bells of the streetcar's coming / By toeing the track I knew / And if I were an old man returning / With my satchel and pork pie hat / I'd hit every jazz joint on Bourbon / And I'd hit every one on Basin after that

The years kept passing as they passed me around / From one state ward to another / Like I was an orphaned shoe from the lost and found / Always missing the other / They gave me a harp last Christmas / And all the nurses took a dance / Lately I've been growing listless / Been dreaming again of the past

I'm wandering down to the banks of the great Big Muddy / Where the shotgun houses stand / I am seven years old and I feel my daddy / Reach out for my hand / While I drew breath no one missed me / So they won't on the day that I cease / Put a sprig of crape jasmine with me / To remind me of New Orleans

I was standing on this sidewalk in 1945 in Jacksonville, Illinois

Jubilee

Words and Music by Mary Chapin Carpenter

I can tell by the way you're walking, you don't want company / I'll let you alone and I'll let you walk on and in your own good time you'll be / Back where the sun can find you, under the wise wishing tree / And with all of them made we'll lie under the shade and call it a jubilee

And I can tell by the way you're talking, that the past isn't letting you go / There's only so long you can take it all on, and then the wrongs gotta be on its own / And when you're ready to leave it behind you, you'll look back and all that you'll see / Is the wreckage and rust that you left in the dust on your way to the jubilee

And I can tell by the way you're listening, that you're still expecting to hear / Your name being called like a summons to all who have failed to account / For their doubts and their fears, they can't add up to much without you / And so if it were just up to me I'd take hold of your hand / Saying come hear the band play your song at the jubilee

And I can tell by the way you're searching, for something you can't even name / That you haven't been able to come to the table, simply glad that you came / When you feel like this try to imagine that we're all like frail boats on the sea / Just scanning the night for that great guiding light announcing the jubilee

And I can tell by the way you're standing with your eyes filling with tears / That it's habit alone that keeps you turning for home, even though your home is right here / Where the people who love you are gathered, under the wise wishing tree / May we all be considered then straight on delivered down to the jubilee

Because the people who love you are waiting, and they'll wait just as long as need be / When we look back and say those were halcyon days / We're talking about jubilee...

Outside Looking In

Words and Music by Mary Chapin Carpenter

Everywhere I see the signs pointing one direction / No more twists or crooked turns leaving room for doubt / Where I used to take the time for quiet and reflection / Now I only hear the noise of what I am without / I see them walking hand in hand and my eyes just want to linger / On those golden wedding bands wrapped around their fingers / By the time I turn away I feel it once again / I'm back in this familiar place, outside looking in

Baby all the tears between us couldn't fill the spaces / And all the words we grasped at, they just fell away / I kept waiting on forgiveness to fix the broken places / But nothing even like it ever came my way / And tonight I drove around and the street came up before me / I took a turn and then I found this old house coming toward me / I heard the sound a heart must make when a memory's caving in / Oh baby what a hungry place, outside looking in

It's the hardest kind of need that never knows a reason / Are we such a lonely breed or just born in a lonely season / Baby it's all in the eyes, it's where the reckoning begins / It's where we linger like a sigh, it's where we long to be pulled in / It's where we learn to say goodbye without saying anything / Just standing on the borderlines, outside looking in

Where Time Stands Still

Words and Music by Mary Chapin Carpenter

Baby where's that place where time stands still / I remember like a lover can / But I forget it like a leaver will / It's no place you can get to by yourself / You've got to love someone and they love you / Time will stop for nothing else / And memory plays tricks on us, the more we cling, the less we trust / And the less we trust the more we hurt / And as time goes on it just gets worse / So baby where's that place where time stood still / Is it under glass inside a frame / Was it over when you had your fill

And here we are with nothing / But this emptiness inside of us / Your smile a fitting, final gesture / Wish I could have loved you better

Baby where's that place where time stands still / I remember like a lover can / But I forget it like a leaver will / It's the first time that you held my hand / It's the smell and the taste and the fear and the thrill / It's everything I understand / And all the things I never will

This Is Love

Words and Music by Mary Chapin Carpenter

If you ever need to hear a voice in the middle of the night / When it seems so black outside that you can't remember light / Ever shone on you or the ones you love in this or another lifetime / And the voice you need to hear is the true and the trusted kind / With a soft, familiar rhythm in these swirling, unsure times / When the waves are lapping in and you're not sure you can swim / Well here's the lifeline / If you ever need to feel a hand take up your own / When you least expect but want it more than you've ever known / Baby here's that hand and baby here's my voice that's calling, this is love, all it ever was and will be / This is love

And if you ever need some proof that time can heal your wounds / Just step inside my heart and walk around these rooms / Where the shadows used to be, you can feel as well as see how peace can hover / Now time's been here to fix what's broken with its power / The love that smashed us both to bits spent its last few hours / Calling out your name, I thought this is the kind of pain / From which we don't recover

But I'm standing here now with my heart held out to you / You would've thought a miracle was all that got us through / Well baby all I know, all I know is I'm still standing / And this is love all it ever was and will be / This is love / And I see you still and there's this catch in my throat and / I just swallow hard 'til it leaves me / There's nothing in this world that can change what we know / Still I know I am here if you ever need me / And this is love

And if you ever think of me let it be around twilight / When the world has settled down and the last round of sunlight / Is waning in the sky, as you sit and watch the night descending / A car will pass out front with lovers at the wheel / A dog will bark out back and children's voices peal / Over and under the air, you've been there lost in the remembering / And if you ever wish for things that are only in the past / Just remember that the wrong things aren't supposed to last / Babe it's over and done and the rest is gonna come when you let it / And this is love, all it ever was and will be / This is love, when you let it, if you let it now / This is love, all it ever was and can be / This is love

Why Walk When You Can Fly

Words and Music by
Mary Chapin Carpenter

Moderately

A cappella

In this world there's a whole lot of trou-ble, ba-by; in this world there's a

whole lot of pain. In this world there's a whole lot of trou-ble, but a

whole lot of ground____ to gain. Why take when you could be

giv - ing? Why watch as the world___ goes by? It's a

hard e- nough life to be liv-ing. Why walk when you___ can fly?

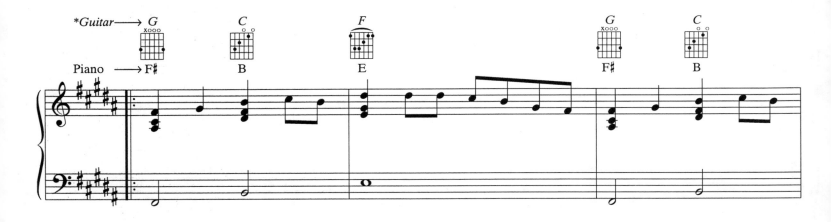

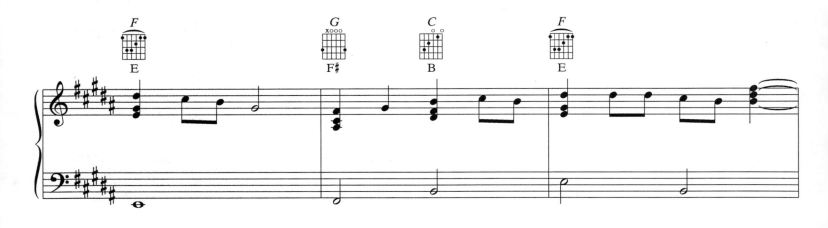

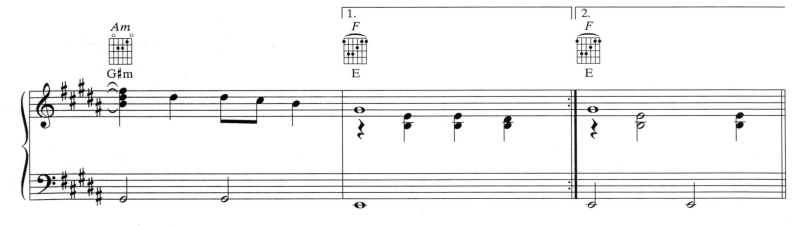

*Guitarists: Tune all strings down a half step.

In this world there's a whole lot of sor - row; in this world____ there's a
In this world there's a whole lot of gold - en; in this world____ there's a

whole lot of shame. In this world____ there's a whole lot of sor - row and a
whole lot of plain. In this world____ you've a soul for a com - pass and a

whole lot of ground____ to gain. When you spend your whole____ life
heart for a pair____ of wings. There's a star on the far ho -

wish - ing, want - ing and won - der - ing why,____ it's a
ri - zon, ris - ing bright in an az - ure sky.____ For the

long e - nough life to be liv - ing. Why walk when you can
rest of the time that you're giv - en, why walk when you can

fly?

15

House Of Cards

Words and Music by
Mary Chapin Carpenter

cards.

When we dream it's of the wind,

blow - ing cold____ and hard.

When we wake up, we____

____ still live____

in a house of cards.____

Repeat and fade

21

Stones In The Road

Words and Music by
Mary Chapin Carpenter

to us _____ to make our way ____ back _____ home.
all those fires, ____ as we raced each oth - er _____
oth - er deal, ____ be -

_____ home. _____

A Keeper For Every Flame

Words and Music by
Mary Chapin Carpenter

She says it's been so long — she can't re-mem-ber when —

the men-tion of his name___ did-n't make her feel a-gain___

that ev - 'ry-thing is pos - si - ble and
some-one in his past___ that he
heart___ had bro - ken, but

ev - 'ry day a brand new start.___
has-n't got-ten o - ver yet.___
it was just a lit - tle bruised.___

Yeah, love's___
Each day's
I thought

let it go.
no one leaves.
how I know.

There's a keep - er for ev - 'ry flame.

To Coda ⊕

1.

F♯m7 **E/G♯** **A** **D A**

D/F♯ **E A** **2. C♯m**

There was

Tender When I Want To Be

Words and Music by
Mary Chapin Carpenter

Moderately fast

I have a heart____ that's proud,____ ____ you bet.____ I have a mind____ that won't____ for - get,

and I have arms____ that are strong____ and yet____ ten - der when they want____ to be.____

Well, you can be the will that finds the way.____

2. Instrumental

You can be the one who saves____ the day,____ but show me ten - der when it's

time____ to say____ ex - act - ly how it ought____ to be.____

34

No, you don't have to take the whole world on,___ just be ten - der when you want to be.___

Sha la la la la la.___

D.S. al Coda

Don't ev - er let me hes - i -tate to be ten - der when I want to be.

Sha la la la la la.

Sha la la la la la.___ Sha la la la la

la la.___

Shut Up And Kiss Me

Words and Music by
Mary Chapin Carpenter

Don't mean to get a lit - tle for - ward____ with you.
Did - n't ex - pect to be in this po - si - tion.
Come____ clos - er, ba - by, I can't____ hear you.

Don't mean to get a - head of
Did - n't ex - pect to have to
Just an - oth - er whis - per,

It's been too long— since some-bod-y whis-pered, ooh,

1.

(Whispered:)
"Shut up and kiss— me." —

2.

(Whispered:)
"Shut up and kiss— me." —

There's some-thing 'bout the si-lent type— at-tract-ing me— to you.—

All bus'-ness, ba - by, none of the hype___ that no___ talk - er can___ live up to.___ Ooh.

Talk is cheap and ba-by, time's ex-pen-sive. So why___ waste an-oth-er

It's been too long___ since___ some-bod - y whis - pered, ooh,___ ooh.___

ooh, "Shut up and kiss___ me."___

Ooh,_____ ooh._____ Ooh._____

"Shut up and kiss___ me."

45

The Last Word

Words and Music by
Mary Chapin Carpenter

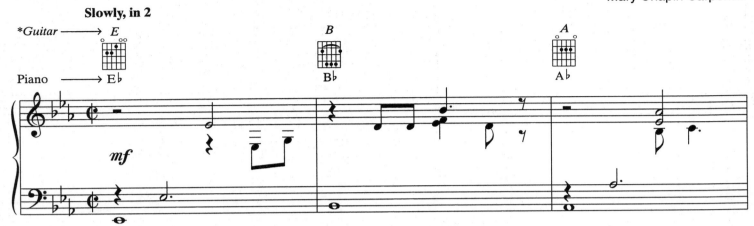

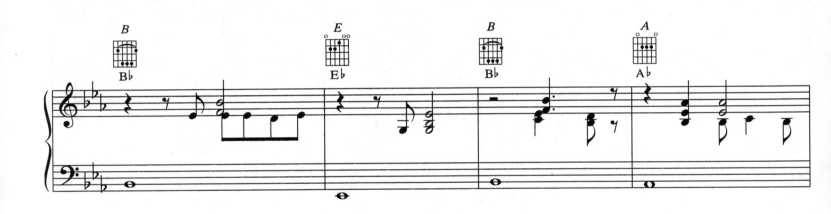

You can have_____ it._____ I don't want_____

*Guitarists: Tune all strings down a half step.

The End Of My Pirate Days

Words and Music by
Mary Chapin Carpenter

sev - en seas. And those___ who search___ for___ treas - ure,

they___ must live___ on grand - er dreams.___ We rose and fell just

like___ the tides.___ He filled my heart and soul, and I_____ bur - ied

all my dreams for some-one else to find in my pi - rate days.___

This world____ is kind - er to____ the kind____ that won't____

____ look back.____ They are____ the cho - sen few____ a-

my____ friend,   since I came____ to the end
my____ friend.   So I came____ to the end

of my pi - rate days.____   of my pi - rate days.____

(Sing 1st time only)

Repeat and fade

Where Time Stands Still

Words and Music by
Mary Chapin Carpenter

And

lov-er can,— but I for-get it like a leav-er—will. It's the first time that you

held my hand; it's the smell,— and the taste,— and the fear,— and the thrill. It's ev-'ry-thing I

un-der-stand and all the things I nev-er will.

Jubilee

Words and Music by
Mary Chapin Carpenter

64

way to the ju - bi - lee.

And I can

tell by the way you're lis - t'ning that you're

still ex - pect - ing to hear your

name be - ing called, like a sum - mons to all who have

failed to ac - count for their doubts————— and their————— fears. They can't————

add up to much with - out————— you. And so

fill - ing with tears,_____ that it's hab - it a - lone keeps you

turn - ing for home,_____ e - ven though your home is right here,

where the peo - ple who love you are gath - ered,_____

un - der the wise wish - ing tree. May we all be con -

sid-ered, then___ straight on de-liv-ered___ down to the ju - bi - lee.

'Cause the peo-ple who love you are wait - ing,___

and they'll wait just as long as need be.___

When we look back and___ say___ those were hal-cy-on

days,   we're talk - ing 'bout___ ju - bi - lee.___

John Doe No. 24

Words and Music by
Mary Chapin Carpenter

1. I was stand-ing on__ this side-walk in

2.–5. *See additional lyrics*

nine-teen for-ty-five__ in Jack - son-ville, Il - li-nois.

When asked__ what my name was, there came no re-ply.__ They said I was a

Additional Lyrics

2. They searched for a mother and they searched for a father,
And they searched till they searched no more.
The doctors put to rest their scientific tests,
And they named me John Doe No. 24.
And they all shook their heads in pity
For a world so silent and dark.
Well, there's no doubt that life's a mystery,
But so too is the human heart.

3. And it was my heart's own perfume
When the crape jasmine bloomed on St. Charles Avenue.
Though I couldn't hear the bells of the streetcars coming,
By toeing the track I knew.
And if I were an old man returning,
With my satchel and pork pie hat,
I'd hit every jazz joint on Bourbon,
And I'd hit every one on Basin after that.

4. The years kept passing as they passed me around
From one state ward to another,
Like I was an orphaned shoe from the lost and found,
Always missing the other.
They gave me a harp last Christmas,
And all the nurses took a dance.
Lately I've been growing listless,
Been dreaming again of the past.

5. I'm wandering down to the banks of the Great Big Muddy
Where the shotgun houses stand.
I am seven years old and I feel my daddy
Reach out for my hand.
While I drew breath no one missed me,
So they won't on the day that I cease.
Put a sprig of crape jasmine with me
To remind me of New Orleans.

This Is Love

Words and Music by
Mary Chapin Carpenter

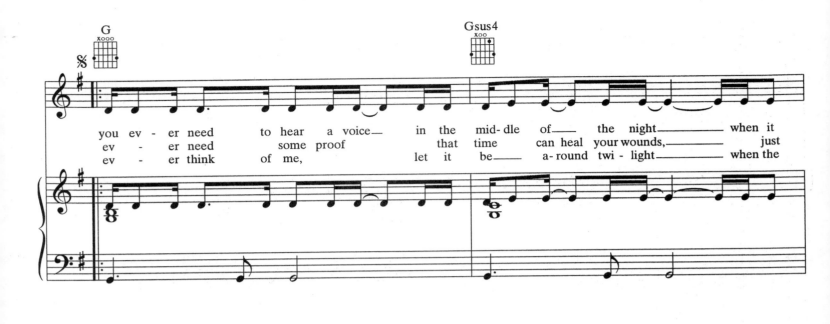

you ev - er need to hear a voice___ in the mid-dle of___ the night___ when it
ev - er need some proof that time can heal your wounds,___ just
ev - er think of me, let it be___ a-round twi - light___ when the

seems so black___ out - side that you can't re - mem - ber light___
step in - side___ my heart and walk___ a - round these rooms;
world has set - tled down and the last___ round of sun -

___ ev - er shone___ on you___ or the ones you love___ in this
where shad-ows used___ to be,___ you can feel as well as see
light is wan - ing in___ the sky, as you sit and watch the

76

are lap - ping in / and you're not____ sure you can swim, well,____
ing out your name; / I thought this____ is the kind of pain____
ver and un - der / the air;____ you've been there, lost

here's the life - line. / If you
from which we don't re - cov - er. / But I'm
in the re - mem - b'ring. / If you

ev - er need to feel a hand____ take up your own when you
stand - ing here now with my heart held out to you. You would - 've
ev - er wish for things that are on - ly in the past, just re -

Csus2

And I —— see you still, —— and there's this catch in my

Dsus4

throat, and I just — swal - low hard —— till it leaves — me.

Csus2

There's noth - ing in this — world that can change what we know.

Dsus4

Still, I know — I am — here if you ev - er need

And this is _____ love. _____

me.

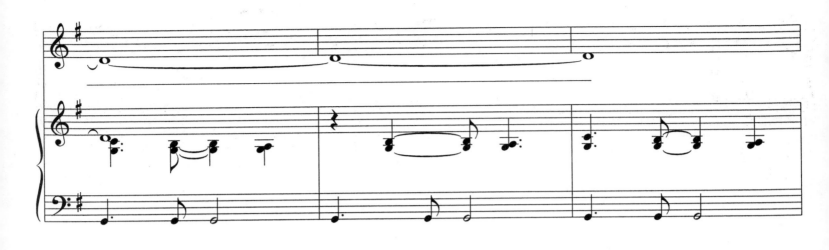

Moderately slow, rubato

Outside Looking In

Words and Music by
Mary Chapin Carpenter

I'm back in this_____ fa - mil - iar place,
Oh ba - by, what_____ a hun - gry place,}
out - side_____

look - ing in._____

Ba - by,